Tumbled Time

Tumbled Time

poems by

Cynthia Linkas

Cover design by Shay Culligan

Cover Photograph by Danielle N. Linkas

ISBN: 978-1-950462-98-8

Kelsay Books Inc.

kelsaybooks.com

502 S 1040 E, A119
American Fork, Utah 84003

for Tom

Acknowledgments

Grateful acknowledgement to the editors of the following publications in which these poems appeared:

Avocet, A Journal of Nature Poems: "Stars," "Imprinted," "All of it Sings You," "Fox," "Heron," "A New Place to Walk," "Yellow Dog," "Barn Owls," "Mated for Life," "Imprinted," "Sea Gifts," "Understory," "Roses," "Stones," "Fireflies," "Avocet," "Angels," "The Art of Trees," "Rack," also called "Spring Walk"

The Aurorean: "Tumbled Time"

Chiron Review: "Amber," "Dad"

Heart, Poetry and Prose: "Glass Bowl"

Pegasus, Nevada: "Epithalamion," "Turtle," "New Rain"

Poem: "A Freshening Wind," "For a Daughter's Birthday"

Time of Singing: "Prayer"

Common Ground Review: "Closing Rockledge in the Fall"

Quill and Parchment Journal: Featured poet, "Seagifts," "Barn Owls," "Closing Rockledge in the Fall"

Tipton Journal: "No Turning Back," "Trains"

Gratitude

For my first teacher, Alan Feldman, Award-Winning Poet, and the most generous wordsmith I know.

Beloved writers: Miriam Weinstein, Patricia Hanlon, Patricia Lorsch, Jeanne Guillemin, Laura Wainwright, Elizabeth Berges, Anne Emerson, Michal Brownell.

And words cannot express my thanks for my brilliant mentors, Sally Ryder Brady and Betsy Seifter.

For *Art on Sunday,* dear friends: George and Penny Wingate, Robert and Patty Hanlon, Tom Linkas, and Anne Pelikan—my listeners.

Tom, my forever love who makes us all strive.

Son, Christopher, daughter, Malina, and daughter-in-law, Danielle, for their constancy and truth—for everything.

Granddaughters, whose musical names are honey on my tongue, each unique and cherished: Sophia Claire, Louisa "Lulu" Chadwick, Alienna Scarlett, Evangeline Cynthia, Solenne Isabella. And for incomparable grandson, Thomas John.

For heart and belief, my fellow teachers, Sister Barbara and Sister Susan.

Sisters, Cathryn Chadwick and Aggie Koutroupas, lifelong friends, Jocelyn Allen and Carol McInnes; and for his faith, family friend, the Reverend-Doctor Daniel E. Hall.

For the invaluable encouragement of poets and editors, Peter Leverich and Charles Portolano of *Avocet, A Journal of Nature Poetry:* for publishing many of the poems that appear in this collection.

For every word, Elizabeth Hall (1942–2002) and Claudia Gallant (1945–2013).

Tumbled Time is about the everyday moments of life; a slow burning search for a spiritual *presence*. I love stories and portraits, and write about creatures, trees, all of nature, family loves, heartaches, joys, loss, and grief. I find hope and solace in the steadfast beauty of the earth.

Contents

The thread of life passed through us
from all the others

Tumbled Time

Sea glass, frosted tracks of time,
ice blue, beer gold,
tossed everywhere on this beach, even under rocks.

Tides turn matter over on itself, even ours.

We touch this glass and mourn
because we know
how life leaves a trail of broken shards, a smoked beauty.

We pocket the bright blue
and all that lies within,
its color and shape and spirit of *once*.

Its new form of *now*.

Avocet

The avocet with spindle legs race the breaking waves,
dart at the froth, dodge and retreat,
their tiny tastes scooped through needle beaks,
their rounded tummies full
of an irrepressible joy.

More endangered every year—
sea on one side, humans on the other,
they stick together—fearless and determined.

When sports teams choose mascots, they think power, speed,
leopard, bear, cheetah,
but for my crucible, I'll stick with the sturdy avocet,
its comical little body, quick-witted retreats,
spirited, tireless work.

The fact that it's still here.

Hands

My grandmother's hands
veined and wrinkled,
skin loose and soft,
fingers reddened and knobby.
I look at mine; they're the same
short, strong fingers, trimmed half moons of nail

but mine are sun-browned, sprinkled with spots.

Oh, give me that tan, those daily walks with the dog,
the cavorting in blue water,
hands sun-kissed by play and fresh air and time.

My grandmother's hands
rarely waved
in ecstatic breezes.
White, dry,
roughened,
they washed the whites in bleach
and stirred great pots of stews and soups,
wielded knives to cut vegetables,
kneaded the dough and at night,
wrapped in a black rosary,
stiff from a day's hard work,
they prayed.

Ferns

For Christopher

On Battle Road at the Minuteman park
where we hiked on weekends
needing to sweat,
in boots and bandannas,
our three year old jumped the rocks, aiming his stick,
voice rising in battle,
in discovery
of each new species, skunk cabbage, curled fern.
Enemy, the redcoat,
Minuteman soldier, ours,
bowl-cut hair blown around his snapping eyes,
he'd pounce, shriek.

And then we'd find the marker, 1775,
number of dead,
English men, Americans, "the shot heard round the world,"
soldiers who fought here, Paul Revere,
dates, green with lichen and time. Our boy,
halted
in the stillness.

Back home, we'd break out apples, juice, beer and cheese,
build a pillow nest, crawl in.

We were the cabbage leaves snuggled in damp wood,
the uncurling ferns in new light, grateful for a soldiers' sacrifice.
And then our boy grew up and was living in Virginia.
And during a visit, he took us to the civil war battlefields,
still drawn
to monuments, and the history of battle,
his grave attention, the same.

Those Minuteman hikes
were in him,
along with the silent, breathing granite,
and its story of blood and bone.

Amber

I have a small rock the color of rich honey
with flecks all through it
that mar its clarity.

Imperfections.

Enhancements.

Like our life
Spilling,
sweet,
sticky

then strong,
formed and
full of light.

Fox

Walking along the straight of the canal,
I catch a flash of red-brown far ahead.
A lost jacket,
A furry shine in the sun.

I hurry, eyes fixed.
Closing in, a tawny body, spray of tail.
A fox?
I inch toward the tall wheaty stalks.

Oh to be the egret white as snow
soaring above all wet, wild mysteries.

It pounces, it's hunting,
I pick up speed.

Stuck in flesh,
dragging my load
of words—luscious fur, pointy nose,
sharp straight ears
leaping into the tall grass
after a muskrat,
a fisher
an otter
the evidence that I saw him, the fox.

Or did I?

For a Daughter's Birthday

for Malina

The night of your birth with its stolen heat,
the moon waning,
late cherry tomatoes drying on the vines,
your Dad backed us out onto our street,
my pains, coming hard.

You'd danced in me all spring
as I sang with hundreds of children,
your tiny ear right up against my guitar.
All summer, the beach had sung under our feet,
your brother's, Dad's and mine.

All that singing
and there you were singing yourself,
fierce and squalling,
porcupine hair, jet black eyes.

They placed you in your father's arms
his tears mixed with yours,
soon to join our family,
your brother, shy as a suitor to meet you,
ready to practice his wit on you.

Vivid full lips, furled,
seashell fingertips.
Soon to turn your strong yell
into fiery song,
to open your arms
to the widest, most challenging work.
But for now, damp from our journey,
in the quiet moment
after all the passion and the pain,
I was what you needed.

The thread of life
passed through us
from all the others,
their heartbeats, yours and mine.

Bright red blossom,
you were what I needed.

Sky

Through a small, rectangular skylight,
white, fast moving clouds
blanket the pale blue sky.

in a blink, the rectangle is gray.

snowy white, teal sky,
quick dark change

but wait, now the blue is back and the movement of white,
and my spirit is flying out the small rectangle of light
the entire space of it, now deep teal and rose.

Sometimes, our frame is small
and to see
to know
we must wait.

Turtle

A new sun lifts the morning chill.
I drink the tranquility even as we stir it,
my crunchy steps
and furry flash of yellow dog whipping his stick.

The long canal of blue water cuts the land into banks,
its breezy surface sheared like the back of a sheep.
Mists hover, pine-tree shadows spill over the bank,
like long dark hair.

A mud-green baby turtle lies on the path
helpless on her back, in a cloud of gnats.
My dog sniffs. I look for a stick to help her.

She chomps the stick! Flips over. The dog backs up.
This tiny turtle commands respect.
What a feisty hold on life!
I nudge her for her own good into the water.

Oh, to be inside her kind of shell
with that wild snap that turns us all gentle.

Yellow dog and I press on.
I take her with me in my heart.

I Could Speak to You There

for Cathy

Last night I watched you swollen with life and had no words,
though if we went back to the attic room
where in the dark, we'd listen for scratches in the walls
through connected child nights,
I could speak to you there.

Cautious one, careful scholar, lithe girl you grew into,
like a brushed line of grace, long hair, shapely sad eyes,
with that ability to gentle anything,
even your panicked goat, Spot.

I could speak to you there
about the way that new life works
like an oyster around *one grain* that contains everything,
that holds within itself cells, bone, spirit, blood,
and the imprints of your forgotten self.

Love begins anew.

You will birth each other.

Glass Bowl

We have a large blue glass bowl
sitting on our kitchen counter,
its fragile shimmer, striped as a flicking bass.
Its lip invites
all manner of things *human,*
carrots, say
rosy apples, and green
tawny pears, pussy willows held with twine
baby booties, matches,
wine bottle corks,
a tiny leather prayer book stolen from a church,
an extra fine rolling ball pen,
and yellow stick'ums from our last fight:

"don't dust my desk"

"you're growing spiders"

"love you so"

Time

for Dan

the space of our actions
illusion of more

our path
over common things
phases of moon
rubble of minutes
on the way
on the song

a line of memory
looped through imagination
bumpy with need
softened by hope

this present moment is all,
a mere conviction of more

only love gathers
time
into *now*

Epithalamion

The room is hushed, all breath is held.
We are each of us the bride again, the groom.
Encircled by loved ones, candlelit faces,
our priest lifts a prayer

and like the shadow of a bird's bright wing
across our gathering,
a shudder of presence brims
over your singular love.

We hear the echo of your tender songs, your heroes'
aims that make us feel and believe.
Now all the work you undertake together widens.

And from a long way out on this high wire called
marriage, your parents,
all of us,
bless you,
leaving our marks of time at the door.

We'll watch the light between you
spill onto your guests,
dance, feast and hold you this night,

remembering how many times we've tumbled
oh, how we've tumbled

Into a net so strong,
so safe, so tightly woven
of the essence of ordinary, wondrous moments

like this one.

Trains

The train to Boston eases out of Penn station
leaving New York where my kids live now.
The city shimmers against a gray sky.
An airplane climbs along at just our speed.

My grand-babies love their wooden trains.
I see them bent over the tracks they've spread
all over the living room rug,
their tiny necks like spring branches on a cherry tree
as they ease the engines into sure arrivals.

Their hungry minds love the motion, the spirits of the engines,
the coal they swallow, their tenders, stories and serious work,
hopes, like ours
the good engine must make the hill,
survive the tunnel.

On my way home from a week with them,
past wheat-colored grass, turquoise rivers,
shirts and pants blowing on a line.

Train wheels clack, whistle screams.
I smell lollipop breath, maple syrup,
Johnson&Johnson shampoo.

Barn Owls

Barn owls mate for life, find each other through hearing;
their noses and eyes, nearly useless.
White-faced, round-eyed, innately smart,
they solve problems, tell time,
never forget the mate's beating heart.

This morning we fold into each others' warmth
the same for forty years, so like the owls.

A chewing mouse can draw the male from a black sky
where he's been hovering on golden wings.
All night, he hunts mice for his mate and young,
his long talons frantic, quivering.
Nothing else will do in nature's scheme.
Without mice, barn owls die.

And when one mate dies, the other spins his head
around over his back, stops hunting. Dies of sorrow.
I think of our own needs like theirs, so embedded, so precise,
that when unmet, we die small deaths.

And of how imprinted we are when we love,
with forever, unassailable marks
inside this warm, known fit of our bodies.

Faith is knowing what you can't quite believe
—Flannery O'Connor

Prayer

Swing out on a rope over a spring river
that boils over sharp rocks
and churns up silt and stunned fish,
their eyes round and staring.

Awaken to its spray.

Hunger for the deep place
of mossy stones and filtered light.

When the rope swings back,
step onto the solid bank.
Then push back out.

Suspended over the rushing river,
graced,
and terrified,
I know

something about who God is.

Snowy walk

On the cold trail in the snow,
I'm inside my down jacket, inside me.
Warm hat low over my ears, I take in
sunlight flickering through frosted firs,
paw prints.
Under icy branches and breezes,
I hail the winter world,
offer thanks for it, grateful for so many things, yet
ask
and ask again for needs, mine and the worlds'.

Slicing the quiet as I walk,
I am an onion coiled into itself, further
and further in.
I am body, spirit,
boots and sweat, exhilarating clouds of breath,
brilliant light and silence.

Silence like no other,
not absence of word or note
but presence,
salt of tears, the burn
strong as incense, as perfect chord.

The Beginning and the End

By night, I drive to the hospital with coffee ice cream
and guide my dying Uncle's hands on the spoon.
He misses his lips, his eyes smile with trust.

By morning, my granddaughter holds her spoon too
fifteen months, ninety-one,
both mouths open like hungry birds.

The beginning and the end.

The baby has a new favorite game—
carries her step stool to the middle of the kitchen,
climbs up, wobbles, stretches her hand out for me.
I show up every time.

White as the pillow, love, naked in his face,
graceful even now, Uncle takes a last shuddering breath.

I see the baby in my kitchen teetering on her stool,
eyes, luminous,
stepping down on her own.
Launched.

The beginning and the end.

Word

flecks of light,
face of moon,

dark sky,
frosty morning,
homey little bird,
snow moist on my hair,
icy branch stuck in a drift,
the shape of a sword

eyes of every hue,
lips and color of voice, so sentient
so new
sinews, lines of song

a full, deep sleep,
hard concentrated work,
stirring harmony
tender touch, too full for speaking,
all these,

And *word*—
in nature, in earth,
holding all
naming all.

Stones

unknowing is a way.
a mind's hunger,
an impediment to be worked around,
like the stones of a spring river, all sizes and shapes,
smooth and ragged,
rush of water over and around
with ingenuity and direction.

quick stir of my heart.

the river's whoosh, its wild free song,
would be silenced
without the stone.

The Canal

Walking in the cool dawn,
the canal teems with unseen life, beneath
and above, the hungry heron with spindle legs, the calm
a long narrow mirror
slicing the brown banks of land, trees
on either side, branches, sticks
pale with green buds, filigreed flickering light.

Love steps out of the shadows

full of a truth we cannot hold but for a moment,
more than this stillness, this beauty

filling every pore and space,
running my heart through

like the long narrow shining canal
and all its depth.

Closing Rockledge in the Fall

Shut off hot water, oil the table
There we are, platters of fish drenched in lemon,
steaming pasta, water in jelly jars, jewel-red wine,
toddler with a tiny fork, buttery lips shiny with smiles.

Haul in kayaks, fold the sails
Tom, Max and Sam push the boundaries, scuba diving
for treasures, Jacques Cousteau.
Sail races, whipping wind in the eyes that smart with freedom,
Beaver Island, brown eyed seals, heaven.

Garden to bed, pepper with shells
Sophia and Shawna on the fiery rocks, long hair shining,
threading designs, beads everywhere, rainbow colors.

Close the flue, secure the storms
Lulu leaps all over the slippery seaweed,
always out beyond where she should be,
spazzing, dancing, irrepressible.

Temp to 55, store the lamps
Alie upside down on the phosphorescent beach, Evie kissed,
Maisie-dog at her feet, Solenne giggling at her fiddler crab,
our littlest ones.

And across the warm, dark lawn—kids fly,
capture the flag,
ghost in the graveyard, amoeba tag
streaks and streaks of kid,
phosphorescent in the moonlight,
deafening shrieks; captured.

Tuck in the beach chairs; wipe down life jackets
Sea glass everywhere, rosy as the setting sun
on gleaming sand in the low low tide.

Six small hands full of treasure, forever in my heart,
Legos; paints; art all over the table
before the renovation
before the years of growing into Rockledge,
a kitchen's bumpy floors
smells of toast and pumpkin bread
and little ones in my arms, singing Pete Seeger songs,
warming on the old back steps
in the morning sun.

Newborn

Five weeks old,
dark blue eyes
lips, the color of pale pink light
that Estee Lauder will never capture,

Arch of brow, line of chin, and all that silken black hair,
a fringe of bangs, yours alone
the turn at your crown
and over the curve at your temple
beside those tiny ears.
A perfect New York haircut.
You frown, yawn, sleepy-smile.

Bright-eyed, grave, you talk to us,
break into toothless throaty laughs

and generations play
in the features of your face

as the dust of stars still clings to you.

New Rain

My grandchildren
spill their laughter and questions,
their songs,
hugs,
nonsense and stories,
tumble through and over my old hurts,
bumping and bouncing all the way down
to where a dry pile of stones,
far under the dirt and grass,
haven't felt the rain
soaking them
in a very long time.

Angels

silver maples ring our yard
white with frost,
one-hundred years standing sentinel,
graceful and forbidding
reminding me of muscular, towering angels

fragile leaves, all manner of green vesture,
blue-black bark like armor
nothing human about them at all

but they explode sparks of care
through quiet witness
and their own language,
wooden layers, soils and depth.

their steadfast roots all intertwined together
give me the courage to rise again at dawn

to know my place in this world too
from which I can enter whatever dark tunnel is given
and discover and speak the just word.

The Art of Trees

A snow globe out the window, perfect white dots
falling and falling, good day
to make art with granddaughters—water color, oil, marker,
collage, mosaic, charcoal,
our favorite to draw is a huge sprawling tree.

Trees are friends with a language all their own,
treeness lives inside our heads.

Our first brush stroke—a fine charcoal line along the bottom
of the large gray paper, wide trunk set into it, grass and flowers.

Then we start the splitting.

Main trunk, cut in two, then in four directions,
each top of a new branch splits again, multiplied until
all of us follow meandering branches, splitting until
we are at the top, there is no more room,
and *tree* is a mass of thick and tiny lines.

Girls' expressions are intent over the page, following splits,
all colors of hair spilling into brown eyes.

Now, the leaves. We place each type of leaf on the myriad of sticks
at the ends of many many splits.
Evie with her light touch, brush-strokes, feathery.
Alie in detailed color and line, each leaf, a new world.
Solie dabs her blots, bold and sure,
drawing the eye to the concept of leaf.

My girls in strokes and breaths,
following branches to their just ends, have drawn
what their little lives truly need—
connective tissue, cooperation, color, beauty, community,

48

cell, micro-organism, each leaf and tiny branch belonging,
reaching, growing, every leaf a brand new thought, and all of them
creating a whole
more than the sum of its parts. They step back.
They know it.

The result is our tree of almost Byzantine beauty.
And an afternoon of stirring love.

Choir

Truly to sing, that is a different breath.
            —Rainer Maria Rilke

The high note is not the only thing.
            —Placido Domingo

We lift our voices on a stirring melody,
a resolution of chord,
and in the precise tuning, the apt release,
gather all our loves in and hold them,
break through conundrum,
face hidden sorrow

and discover, in song and text, an inner calm
in this chaotic world.

Through counterpoint and texture our conductor leads us,

on a bright rim of reason,

a deep nerve of feeling,

neither solely through reason
nor feeling, nor doubt

but in the light and dark of the community of chord,

and a haunting solo voice.

Grandchild

Cold from the raw spring air,
you climbed into my lap, slipped
your fingers under my arms. "You're so warm," you said
and I held all four years of you.

You whispered, eyes solemn,
"My Mom and Dad don't hold me sometimes,"
telling on your parents.

I laughed out loud.
Right then, they had three babies under four.

"It's their job to make you brave," I said,
"to teach you strength.
And mine, to hold you."

"What about the others?" you asked. "You don't have room."

"Oh I do. The heart expands, that is love.
I'll welcome all the new worlds that come.

But for now, it's my job to hold *you,*
all long legs, elbows and knees of you,

in every way,
for as long as I have."

Mated for Life

This morning on the pond,
a pair of swans skim a flat gray surface
brooding in fog, beaks low,
necks like clefs on a staff,
their glide preternaturally calm.

The male's wings enclose
his under-feathers, soft
inside a muscular cape
a whorl of silence.

The female's wings flutter,
lift from her sides.
She wants to crack open
his order and balance, his tranquil beauty,
break through silence,
soar above the oily shine,
the pale pink lily pads, the smear of homely pond.

He swirls in the other direction
and she patterns his arc,
stirring the water in parallel rims
like fine arched eyebrows.

Sea gifts

Wind rattles the windows of our cottage.
Children and grandchildren, back to their lives; holiday, done.
A good fire blazes and outside, wind wrinkles the sea
like the casual silk of my holiday blouse,
covered by a purple owl apron,
Lulu's gift that I love.

I'm thinking about our gifts to each other,

step out on the porch—sliver of moon,
pinpoints of light, a brilliant, cold Maine sky.
The holidays are fraught and wondrous,
we humans and our anxious giving.

In the dark below the rock ledge, waves shush in a high tide.
And I know that in the morning
seaglass will be strewn everywhere down there,
even under rocks
frosted colored jewels, shiny coal,
shards of clay from ships' pots, sunken treasures,
here, in front of our cottage
and nowhere else along this shore
the wonder of it.

All summer, boats pull up
beach-comers hold paper cups for gathering.
Jars-full adorn our mantle,
our children make wreaths, bracelets,
frames and art.
And the tide gives
whether we are here or not
every day,
new secrets and history,

washed up beauty,
gifts.
If you can see them.

Wings

At a memorial for my friend, Holly
in a room surrounded by her art,
I stand before her woodcuts
of majestic angels
enormous, principled beings
in their soaring, whirling muscular flight,
devil-fighting angels from Paradise
whose wings cover us humans in their protective span.

Gentle Holly, her small arms and long fingers chiseled
the hard wood to a physical permanence of her vision.

As I walk the snowy trails each day,
hovering, ghostly watchers of our world whisper
from the tops of white-capped firs,
from under the blanket of white,
in the mystery of the hollow tree nest,
the small, deep hole in the snow,

and bid me to carve into my own hard wood

which is words.

Racks

Walking along a mossy stone wall,
limbs loosening,
dots of orange interspersed among pale gray leaves,

some hunters have lined up racks of antlers,
prizes for the good shots
dancing among the stones.

I climb up over a rise,
to my left, the blue sea, frosty sprinkling of whitecap,
to the right in a neat valley,

something brown lies in the sand

belly down, spindly legs folded under, nose in chest,
his rack buried.

Oh he's dead.

I stop and mourn and picture the row of racks along the wall.

Then he leaps up
and flies over the goldenrod,
white tail flickering in the brush,

waking up my ruins
my small words, up and over the scrubs of pine,
red berries and shades of green

my words, plans

puckish with new life.

Gathering in

There is a trail out behind our house
with its same low wet places,
its curve to the pond
where I'm held and healed and
can often remember
shadows and loss, purity and bliss,
wrestling and fears
and no guarantees.

I walk that country with my sweet, white dog.

Crystalline breezes play over nature's pruned branches
and strong ones that high winds have bent low.

I gather into me the scrub brush, giant fir, oak, maples
the intertwining roots that bore down deep
and steady each other for a hundred years
in a steadfast reach for the stars.

Understory

I've returned to a cottage on an island, tucked into a safe cove
where years ago my sunny children swam
and spread their lunches onto the nooks of boulders.

Now the lonely gulls and I perch on my favorite gray rock.
A lone cormorant plunges and the rippled sea is tinged with rose.

The tip of a fin slices the surface of the water.
The gulls stiffen beside me.
There it is again piercing the shine,
a supple dorsal fin, eight feet from the rock,
a fin lithe and infused with calm, carving a path.

By noon, the word is out. A fifteen foot great white shark,
lost, stuck in the cove. Biologists flood the island.
She makes the evening news.
Sympathizers arrive in blow-up boats to get a glimpse
and feed her, and commiserate.
The coast guard forms a barrier against the fools.

For days, I come to the rock.
They place a microchip in her smooth back,
discuss a plan to lead her to the sea.
Once, I see her wide mouth and rows of teeth as she swims up.

There—my little girl reads on her float, sunhat shading her face,
tips of her braids submerged along with Judy Blume.
And there—my son's carved limbs against the light,
poised on the high rocks
of our quiet cove,
adults now with children of their own to keep safe.

I think of all that can turn dark, and yet
with an earthly beauty, full of carved light,

and all that lies below the surface,
hidden mysteries,
life's understory.

Feather and Air

I love the birds that come and inspect my feeder
to see if I refilled it yet
their tiny bodies all feather and air
beaks the size of holes in the feeder bags
finches in pairs and threes
their nervous games
like middle schoolers on the playground.

Thank goodness for the more substantial tube
with its larger holes
for big guys,
woodpeckers, cardinals, mourning doves,
with their wide flight patterns from the trees.

I wonder
do they pick up cues?
who goes where
who's biggest, who to stay away from
who's bravest, kindest,
who to emulate, to trust, to put in its place.

Suddenly they all grow close.

It's the cat.

I run out in my slippers in the spring muck.

No Turning Back

There's no turning back after the sung note shimmers
into a hushed audience.

After you step into someone's life and break open its mysteries,
and knit them with yours,

After you've lost your ruby ring
where you'd been furiously picking-your-own ripe red tomatoes.

All summer, we spooned treats into the delphiniums.
They stood side by side and tall,
singing out that purply blue, feathery white,
iced blueberry, and the palest of lavenders
that no painter in all his genius can ever capture.

Then our huge yellow dog took a nap
on top of the vibrant, blooming bed.

Girls

From the top of the long staircase
they pause in a row
in cotton dresses,
daughter
and three little girls
following like ducklings,

from pale white skin
to coffee colored, luscious, creamy,
and all the colors of hair, brunette, blond curls,
straight black,
dark eyes all snappy, playful
and their mother, still a beauty

and they make their way down the stairs
into the living room,
tumbling over one another,
singing White Coral Bells,
a gaggle, a bevy,

a miracle of girls.

All of it Sings You

After the snow melts,
ridges of rock, dusty with sleep,
mosses, mudded over with crushed leaves,
thirst for a first slashing rain
to freshen, sweep it clean

all of it sings you

Once, I sought you
in texts and liturgies,
lone voiced chants,
praying the ancient rituals,
giving the impression that I knew
what to do
about you

all of it sings you

Now, lying on my back on a dew-stung spider's web
under a field of pale morning stars, caught wordless, prayerless,
thoughtless in a silent swim of light

still, all of it sings you

Round and round the rim of the sorrow

The Surest Thing

At low tide on the rosy beach
Tommy and his sisters search for seaglass.
It is everywhere.

"Why?" he asks.
"The waves," says Sophia, "sunken ships, people's bottles."
"Is it trash?" asks Tommy.
"Beauty," says Lulu, twirling in a pink puddle.

Sophia leaps over the big rock. "I have to find a bright blue!"
"No going over there," shouts Tommy. "It's the rule."

In the seaweed, a sugary aqua.
Near his toe, almost hidden under a rock, a bright blue.
He glances at the big rock.
He pockets the blue.

Shadows lengthen on the gleaming sand.
Their mother calls.
"Coming," they cry like seagulls.

Sophia runs across the beach, her pail full of colors.
"What will you do with it?" asks Tommy, fingering his blue.

At the cottage she tapes four pieces to a window.
"Light will shine through it," she says.
"The sea makes it out of trash," he says.
She tapes eight more, then twelve.
"There's a hole in the middle," he says.
"I know," Sophia sighs. "I have to find bright blue."
He fingers the sea glass in his pocket.
It's rare. He didn't have to go over the big rock to find it either.

The family sits down.
Lulu dumps her glass on a plate, a centerpiece.
"A color hill," she laughs. Her colors dance in the candlelight.
"What a pretty window pattern," says Mom. "It has a hole in it,"
says Dad.

Tommy watches his sister's sad smile.
"Here," he says. He slides it over to her.
She gasps. It is truly rare, shining like a sapphire.

"Tomorrow's tide will bring more." Tommy shrugs.
"It's the surest thing I know."

Dad

When he left us, it was slow.
He'd careen down the hospital hall,
a dried out empty rain-stick, listing to the right.

We could have poured beans in him
to make a rustling music.
He'd have liked that,
jerking his head back in mock surprise.
There was just a faint light left in his eyes
yet a song still rising in his heart,
searching day and night for his wife, his love.
She was right there beside him.
He didn't remember her.

All he had, he'd given to us.

In the end, he hoarded food in his cheeks
like a little squirrel, facing a frost.

Roses

On this bitter winter day, we pass a rose garden.
Yellow dog sniffs the bushes wrapped in burlap, capped in snow.

Last spring, in boxes delivered UPS,
they crowded the neighbor's doorway,
strained her front yard.

All summer, petal swirls drew our hunger for color
for scents on the breeze,
fragrant blooms,
hidden, complex folds, rich colors of their blood—
orange moons, rosy evening pales.

Now we remember and almost believe
this core of truth:
They will push out again through spring mud,
and ravish us once more,
halt us in our tracks
to touch a silken mystery.

Like our loved ones gone,
they gather a dormant beauty,
and all the secrets of this life,
waiting.

Une Souche (the stubborn root)

February days turn slowly,
our hills are yellow with thirst.
Trees trimmed or gone
house tired, its regal lines, stark.

This winter, you have been ill,
frail, fighting,
you, *une souche,* the stump
our French forebears had the devil of a time digging up,
after the tree fell.

Tough and trusted root, you hold us all
like the silver maples that edge our lawn
with their unshakable tenure.

Dear, spirited lady that I am blessed to call Mom,
with your feisty, stubborn energy.

I brush the thick and tangled winter vines,
strain to hear the sparrow's chipping song
announcing that this cold heartache will pass,

that your knotty questions and open arms
will still be with us then.

Stars

One night in Canada
we are talking about everything.

Everything but the certainty of your death,
round and round the rim of the sorrow
and our fear of parting.

We fall onto our backs on the worn, wooden dock,
silenced
by a million stars,
bright and alive across the sky.

And for a second, we know
that love is not limited to this moment.

It is not in us.
We are in it.

And the night sky is swathed in flecks of light.

It is our first comfort
since we understood
that you would go.

Heron

On daily walks, we shared the quiet
with a pair of herons. They'd glide in for a landing
like holy ghosts
on the ribbon of the canal, majestic, dusk blue,
with wide, elegant wings.

Built for flight, not earth,
they worked the edge with splatted steps on spindle legs,
long craning necks and needle beaks, slurping fish.
They were our fellows.

On the morning you died,
family around your stark white bed,
throat too tight for words, for prayer,
our heron winging.

Battle, lost. Breaths slowing,
your grace and power lifted up from the broken body,
the quicksilver mind, strong sure limbs, all rising.

And the great blue heron hovered there
in the splintered light,

then soared up with you into a file of snowy clouds.

Imprinted

Five deer appear in the distance,
black against the wheat grass,
buff among dark leaves,
a problem these days.

Yet walking on the canal today
I'm stilled at the sight,
imprinted with awe.

At my feet, star flowers press up through snow
in a warming breeze,
white, sturdy and new.

Star flowers spotted with mud
soiled points of tiny stars
pinning my heart to you

to our walks here and survivals

to the improbability of spring
when bitter wind holds us in its grip

to the imprint of star flowers
pushing up through the mud.

Yellow Dog

Handsome, big-chested beast,
eyes, round and brown.

We walked in the woods
on beaches
and along a canal; he'd find the biggest sticks,
knock me in the head, a goofball dog.

One day on the trail, yellow dog screeched to a stop.
Our gray cat lay dead across the path, still warm. Coyote?
Fisher cat?
My playful dog sat down in the trail, lowered his head
and growled.
A warning, or fury?
Sorrow for the cat.

He wasn't one for hugs with his big dog pride.
But sometimes he'd find me sitting on the floor in tears.
And people, take a lesson from him.
What do you do when someone's grieving?

Keep watch.
Circle with worried eyes, mute, knowing.
Come in close,
touch foreheads.

The Color of Pale Rust

I walk along the canal, long, straight,
spring melt turning it the color of pale rust,
the color of your face during
those last breaths.
I asked the nurse to help us
clear away tubes, oxygen, needles
to wash away the pain
with warm water and lavender soap,
a last assurance of love.

A white egret fishes at the edge
in water the color of rain
and of your eyes.
I watch her slow plod, so unlike the smooth glide of her wings.

We washed the carved line above your brow, deep-set closed eyes,
thick hair
firm bones, full lips,
line of shoulder
hard-worked hands, limbs

I meant to understand *the stillness,*
the color of pale rust,
To know, a word beloved by us.
While ahead on the trail,
the white egret bends her graceful head.

Space

This morning, a winter thaw smoothed the canal
where I walk now without you

the lacy branches,
reflected through a mist,
gathered up the pale new light.

I could feel
you
walking beside me

and between us,
all the years of beauty we took in together

that made a space of us

and in me now

to hold all the sorrow.

A New Place to Walk

In the thick of the winter,
I found a new place to walk.
Far away from laurel branches coated with ice,
crusted, known paths,
bare, shadowy birches bringing you back
making me weep.

I found some miles of straight along a canal,
mine alone
icy, narrow, melting now in pencil lines,
a music staff,
a sorrow song.
Here, the mushy sunlit snow is pure along the bank,
bluish-white waves of it, miles of melting white
and small paw-prints back and forth
across the snow,
the nightly work of coyotes,
fox,
and scurrying mice.

The thrust of life.

A Freshening Wind

I walked over spring green fields, rocky in folds.
A stag and his young stood feeding on the mound,
scents of fur, rich earth, new grass.

The stag lifted his eyes.

You came to me
in a body healed, restored.
My grief folded under me in the grass.

We kept a still company, three deer and me.

A red-winged blackbird washed itself on a branch of
bittersweet.

Then three sharp noses turned together at once
in a freshening wind.

And they leaped off

and took you with them.

Fireflies

he loves silence, can be silent for hours.
his interior is rich, rational and incisive
I would go crazy and try to get him to talk to me

illness has taken our language away
and there is left another kind of love,
like the coursing of blood through veins
like one skin stretched over two beings

once when we were very young, not yet wed,
he took me to his parents' home in the Midwest
and one dark hot night, made love to me in the garden
in a woody patch where he'd played cowboys.
It teamed with hot chirps and blinking fireflies
and we whispered and giggled in glorious transgression.
our love was forever....

all these years, he overwhelmed me,
tireless, voracious, tender,
he needed my flesh,
I thought I needed his spirit more
and didn't know that they were the same.

the heart thinks, the mind feels

sparks rise,
fireflies,
my longing for his body

About the Author

Cynthia Linkas publishes poems in literary journals, especially *The Aurorean, Poem,* and *The Avocet, A Journal of Nature Poetry.* Her short story, *Baggage,* won the PEN Syndicated Fiction contest, was published nationally, and read aloud on NPR's The Sound of Writing. Her novel, *The Roller Palace,* was one of five finalists for the Midlist Press Competition and shortlisted by Tupelo Press. A professional singer and lifelong music teacher, she especially loves Renaissance choral music. She has performed for years with Convivium Musicum of Boston and the Christ Church Choir of Hamilton-Wenham, Massachusetts.